Cliffe Hill

The walk around **New Cliffe Hill Quarry and Billa Barra Hill** will guide you through almost 600 million years of geological time, and 110 years of quarrying history. It will tell an exciting story of volcanoes and earthquakes, the extremes of deserts and glaciers, and will introduce you to some of the oldest signs of life on earth. You will see a 'slice' through Precambrian and Triassic rocks in the vertical quarry faces and view large-scale three-dimensional geological features from a distance.

This route will take you on a walk through the north-west Leicestershire Coalfield, an area that has a strong industrial character with rolling agricultural land woven between quarrying sites and new business parks. Large and small scale planting by the National Forest Company is helping to transform this once sparsely wooded landscape into an attractive area in which to walk, live and work.

The leaflet provides a full description of the route, but it may also be useful to use Ordnance Survey Explorer map number 245 'The National Forest'. Numbers **(1)** to **(10)** in **bold** within the text correspond to specific locations along the walk — please refer to the route map for guidance.

Aerial photograph of New Cliffe Hill Quarry.

Midland Quarry Products

Midland Quarry Products (MQP) was formed in December 1996 and is one of the UK's leading producers and suppliers of hard rock and asphalt. The company operates two quarries and five asphalt plants in the East and West Midlands, the largest of which is the environmental award-winning Cliffe Hill Quarry.

Completion of the Joskin Tunnel

Cliffe Hill consists of two quarries — 'New' Cliffe Hill is an active working quarry with two asphalt plants on site, a railway line and a newly opened tunnel link to the 'Old' quarry. Operations commenced at New Cliffe Hill in the late 1980s, but quarrying has gone on at Old Cliffe Hill since the 19th century. New Cliffe Hill currently produces 4.5 million tonnes of crushed granite aggregate per year (the 'granite' is more technically named the *South Charnwood Diorite*). It is used mainly in the Midlands, south-east England and East Anglia for road and railway construction. Reserves will probably be extracted from New Cliffe Hill until 2005.

In 2002, work began on the construction of an underground tunnel to connect the Old and New Cliffe Hill quarries. This will allow the Company to work the remaining reserves at Old Cliffe Hill, and return them through the new tunnel for processing at the New Cliffe Hill plant. Once re-opened, it is hoped that Old Cliffe Hill Quarry will operate until 2016. The tunnel itself was officially opened in September 2003, and is 9 m wide, 6 m high and 725 m long. It was aptly christened the *Joskin Tunnel* as a result of the naming competition held in the nearby village of Stanton under Bardon. This is a local name, taken from the Joskins Cottages, which used to be located at the northern end of the village.

© Midland Quarry Products Ltd

The Joskin Tunnel entrance.

Did you know…

That approximately 50 tonnes of aggregates are used to construct a house……
The construction of the new stadium for Leicester City Football Club used 45 000 tonnes of aggregate and 5000 tonnes of asphalt……
Aggregates are used in the beer and wine making process to neutralise acids….
They are also added to toothpaste as a good source of calcium!

A bit of history...

Old Cliffe Hill Quarry was bought by a Mr J R Fitzmaurice in 1891; at that time the quarry was worked on a small-scale for the production of stone setts and kerbs. The 'Markfieldite' diorite had a good reputation as a hard-wearing stone, and Cliffe Hill Quarry provided kerb stones to cities in the Midlands and London until the 1950s.

"LET ME BOOK SUPPLIES NOW"

Mr Fitzmaurice installed a manager at the quarry, a Mr Preston. He was interviewed at the quarry site with both men sitting on small heaps of stone. Mr Preston apparently accepted a wage of £3 per week, good going by standards of the day!

Rock drilling in those days was carried out by steam-driven drills, with secondary drilling completed by hand. Steam was provided to the drills from the old traction engine that transported drilling equipment from one face to another.

Picked by a Robot Hand!

Hand drilling was a dangerous and laborious job; a boy would hold a short drill with both hands while a quarryman would hit the drill with a sledgehammer. The boy would turn the drill slightly, and the man would hit it again. This procedure would be repeated until the stone could be split with plugs of steel.

Miss Cliffe

Cliffe Hill Granite Company vans line up in Old Cliffe Hill Quarry.......

A BIT OF HISTORY

In 1894, the Company secured its first big railway contract for 5000 tonnes, and on the 1st of November 1894 the 'Cliffe Hill Granite Company Ltd' was formed. As the demand for products increased the decision was made to install a light railway and to buy some locomotives and wagons. The first locomotive was bought in 1896 and was imaginatively christened *Cliffe*. *Isabel* and *Rocket* joined *Cliffe* over the next few years, and served to haul stone to the crushers and to the sidings.

Company actively encourages community involvement and supports many local projects. A quarry liaison committee meets every three months to discuss and resolve any issues regarding the quarry, and produces a regular publication the *Cliffe Hill Chronicle* to keep local residents up to date with quarry activities.

Mr Preston and family 1899

Picked by a Robot Hand!

CLIFFE HILL GRANITE CO.

The Fitzmaurice and Preston families jointly managed the Cliffe Hill Granite Company for 72 years, until The Tarmac Group plc acquired the company in 1965. The Company then became part of Midland Quarry Products Ltd in 1996. Cliffe Hill has since won many awards for its attention to the environment and the

Driller, Old Cliffe Hill Quarry.

……. As do the trucks!

Geology

The rocks of Charnwood Forest are some of the oldest in England and Wales. They contain unique fossils, the *Ediacaran fauna*, dated as late Precambrian, around 543 to 580 million years old. Similar fossils have also been found at sites in southern Australia, Newfoundland, Russia, China and Namibia. They represent a stage in the formation of life on earth, before sea creatures had evolved shells, as there were no carnivores to prey upon them. It is difficult to compare the Precambrian fossils to present-day organisms, but some of them do resemble modern sea-pens, sea anemones, corals and jellyfish.

Geologists divide the Charnian Supergroup (Table 1) rocks into three groups, the Blackbrook, Maplewell and Brand Groups. The oldest rocks in the area belong to the **Blackbrook Group**, formed when volcanoes erupted large volumes of ash and pyroclastic debris into the air. This material rained down from the sky and settled out in the shallow sea around the volcanoes. The volcanoes are thought to have formed an **island**

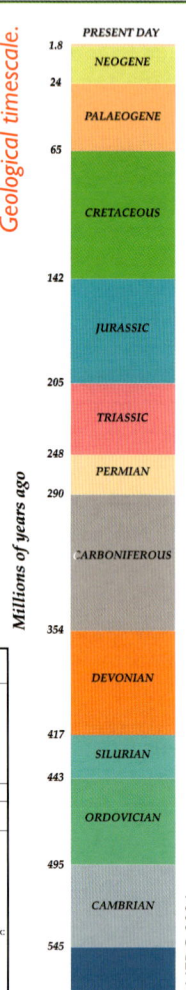

Table 1 Lithostratigraphy of the Charnian Supergroup (Carney et al, 2001).
Nb: Groups, Formations and Members highlighted in red are encountered on this walk.

frond

A typical Ediacaran organism — *Charniodiscus*

disc

fossilised 'frond'

BGS © NERC 2004

Line drawing by John Martin

arc similar to that of Japan today. The volcanic ash, mixed with silt and sand that had been eroded from emergent volcanoes, built up a great thickness of **volcaniclastic** sediments. Burial beneath this great weight compressed the sediments into a hard, **lithified** rock.

Rocks of the **Maplewell Group** were created during a time of violent and almost continuous volcanic eruptions and explosions; lava and large blocks of volcanic rock as well as huge amounts of ash and dust were blasted from the volcanoes to the north-west to settle out as sediments in the surrounding sea. When such sediments are preserved as rocks, they are known as **tuffs** (composed of volcanic ash, cemented into a solid rock) and **volcanic breccias** (made up of a mixture of angular volcanic rock fragments). It is thought that the type of Precambrian volcanic activity may have been similar to the eruptions seen recently on the Caribbean island of Montserrat. Earthquakes related to the volcanic activity caused avalanches and slumping of this sediment down submarine slopes, causing further mixing and upheaval of the jumbled deposits. The semi-consolidated sediments were greatly deformed as blocks and layers were wrenched apart and rolled up like plasticine. The *Sliding Stone Slump Breccia*, an important marker horizon in Charnwood Forest, represents an entire slumping event; a good exposure of the breccia can be seen at Bradgate Park. **For further information please see 'A Geological Walk around Bradgate Park and Swithland Wood' (this series).**

Volcanic eruption on the island of Montserrat (2003).

Another type of rock that outcrops in Charnwood Forest, and is especially well seen at Cliffe Hill is the **South Charnwood Diorite**, known previously as *Markfieldite* after the village of Markfield nearby. The molten diorite is thought to have intruded into the older Charnian rocks, where it cooled down and crystallised into a very hard **igneous** rock. The diorite has been extensively quarried for road and rail aggregate, as well as kerb stones and building stones for local houses and churches; operations are still underway today at New Cliffe Hill Quarry. The precise age of the *South Charnwood Diorite* is not known, but the petrography and geochemistry of the rock is similar to the granophyric diorite at Judkins' Quarry,

8 GEOLOGY

A cross-section through the Precambrian volcanoes of Charnwood Forest, around 600 million years ago.

Nuneaton, which is dated at approximately 603 million years old. This evidence suggests that the volcaniclastic sediments of the Charnian Supergroup described above are therefore older than 603 million years.

The Charnian rocks were then compressed and folded into a large arch-shaped **anticline** structure. The top of the anticline was eroded away to reveal a core of older rocks belonging to the

Blackbrook Group. On a map, the anticline has the appearance of an enormous U-shape orientated NW–SE, with older rocks in the centre, grading outwards into younger rocks. The diorite described above was intruded before the Charnian rocks were folded into this anticline, as the diorite contains **shear zones** that were created during the folding event.

After the Precambrian Period, Charnwood was buried by sediments of **Cambrian** age. By **Triassic** times, some 208 to 245 million years ago, the Cambrian rocks had been eroded away, and a dry, arid **desert** environment prevailed. The crags of Precambrian rock that formed the landscape of the Triassic desert were gradually buried beneath a large accumulation of red breccia, sandstone and lime-rich mudstone or marl (the *Mercia Mudstone* at Cliffe Hill Quarry). Steep-sided river valleys, known as **wadis**, cut in the Precambrian rocks were gradually filled in with younger Triassic sediments that eventually blanketed the area. The Triassic sediment cover accounts for the more gentle rolling landscape between the rugged outcrops of ancient Precambrian rock. An excellent example of a wadi, or 'palaeovalley' can be seen at New Cliffe Hill today.

The Charnian peaks were again partly uncovered or **exhumed** by erosion of the Triassic rocks during the **Tertiary** period. They suffered a final phase of erosion and deposition during the great Ice Age, a period of time known as the **Pleistocene**. Glaciers and ice sheets from the north spread southwards to cover most of Britain, as far south as London, until they melted around 120 000 years ago. Charnwood was covered by ice at least twice, during which time the glaciers eroded large amounts of the Triassic rocks that covered the Precambrian outcrops. Today, the remnants of the Precambrian and Triassic rocks are overlain by deposits of glacial boulder clay, scree and rock-waste (or *head* deposits) and chalky till.

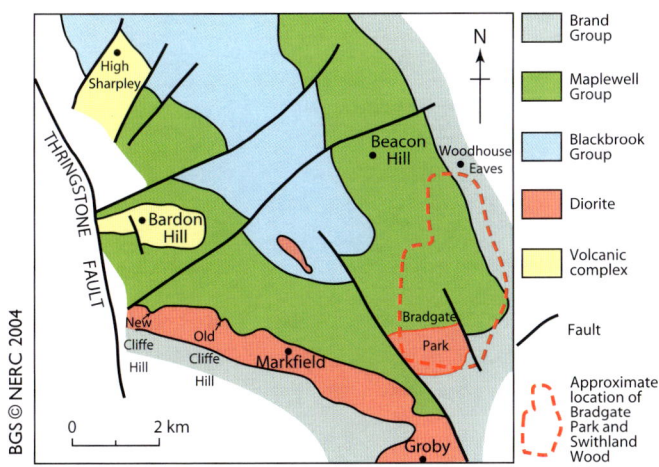

Simplified geological map of the Precambrian rocks of Charnwood Forest. The outcrop pattern defines an open, U-shaped anticlinal structure.

The Walks

Billa Barra Hill

Billa Barra Hill, New and Old Cliffe Hill Quarry A circular walk of about 4.5 km with longer and shorter alternatives, taking approximately 2 to 3 hours.

The entrance to Billa Barra Hill Local Nature Reserve.

BILLA BARRA HILL

The walk starts from the car park at Billa Barra Hill Local Nature Reserve, Billa Barra Lane, near Stanton Under Bardon (1).

How to get there

By car – To the car park at Billa Barra. Exit the M1 at junction 22 and take the A511 towards Coalville and Ashby. Turn left at the first roundabout (there is a service station on left hand side) into Stanton Lane. After approximately 600 m turn right onto Billa Barra Lane, and immediately right on to the car park.

By bus – Call Traveline on 0870 608 2608 for 24-hour travel information.

Billa Barra Local Nature Reserve

is a 19 hectare site, purchased by Hinckley and Bosworth Borough Council in 1996 with grant aid from the National Forest Company, and land donated by The Tarmac Group. The hill-top is a Regionally Important Geological Site (RIGS), with outcrops of the *Bradgate Formation*, the uppermost unit of the *Maplewell Group* (Table 1) described earlier. It is also very interesting ecologically with acid grassland and an old conifer plantation. The site also supports a variety of species, including a rare type of lichen, only found at one other site in Leicestershire. The improved grassland slopes below the gorse scrub line are planted with more than 10 000 native broadleaved trees, which will be used to harvest tree seeds of local provenance.

You may like to start the Cliffe Hill walk with a quick tour of Billa Barra Hill. There is an interpretation board at the gate to the site, and a leaflet providing more information is available from Hinckley and Bosworth Borough Council. Walk through the gate and follow the path uphill towards the trees. Pleasant views are to be had all around Billa Barra Hill; you can see Bardon Hill in the distance to the north (the hill with radio masts). The rocks of the Whitwick–Bardon area are thought to be closest to the location of the eruptive volcanic centre in Precambrian times, as the thickest outcrops of dacite are to be found here.

When you arrive at the top of the hill, take the path off to the left, in front of the National Forest bench, and follow this track until you meet a wooden fence. Go through the gate to see the small water-filled quarry **(2)**; a second interpretation board gives you more information on the Billa Barra site. The outcrop consists of well-bedded, fine- to coarse-grained pinkish red volcaniclastic sandstone, with interbedded thinly laminated siltstone and mudstone. You may see sets

A welcome rest! A National Forest bench at the top of Billa Barra Hill.

of cross-bedding in the sandstone horizons if you look closely. This is the *Bradgate Tuff Formation* of the *Maplewell Group* described earlier. Occasionally you will see that the laminations in the sandstones are disrupted, contorted and folded; they are **syn-sedimentary structures** which indicate that deformation took place during or shortly after deposition of the sediment.

Continue on past the small quarry and walk down the steep hill, taking the wooden steps that lead down to the floor of a second, larger quarry to the northwest (there are often crops of wild blackberries to pick in the summer). It is interesting to note that in the past the quarries at Billa Barra supplied stone to build local drystone walls. On first entering the quarry, you will immediately see a low-angle (almost horizontal) fault surface covered with slickenside groove lineations.

There are also lots of quartz veins at 90° to the slickensides. The fault appears to be parallel to the bedding surfaces observed in the rest of the outcrop, indicating that the fault may be the result of flexural slip between bedding planes. Quartz-filled **en echelon** tension gashes also cross cut the fault surface. You will also notice that the sandstones in this quarry are crossed by numerous joint surfaces, giving them a blocky appearance. The outcrops in this quarry allow us to gain an insight into the lithology of the *Bradgate Formation*, which can be seen at Old and New Cliffe Hill Quarry, but only from afar!

Explore at will around the Billa Barra site, perhaps stop and have a picnic or drink, enjoying the pleasant views around the area. When you are ready, make your way back downhill to the wooden gate. As you leave the car park, turn right on to Billa Barra Lane and walk uphill. After

The small quarry at Billa Barra Hill.

a few 100 m's (opposite Billa Barra Cottage), you may catch glimpses of a small ditch running parallel to the road in the trees to your right; this is all that remains of an old dismantled tramway that transported aggregate between Old Cliffe Hill Quarry and the junction at Bagworth.

Continue past Billa Barra Cottage, set back on your left, and after approximately 100 m, take the footpath on your left, passing two brick cottages on your right. Continue downhill through the trees, and notice the Cliffe Hill Quarry blasting times displayed on the left. Walk up to a small wooden footbridge (over a small, often dry stream in front of you).

Another interpretation board on the right provides information on the type of trees planted around the quarry edges by Midland Quarry Products as part of a National Forest landscaping scheme. Cross over the footbridge and walk uphill to the right, through the recently planted avenue of holly trees — more evidence of planting in the area. The present landscaping scheme has planted more than 60 000 trees around Cliffe Hill Quarry.

The way-marker disc on the wooden post advertises that this footpath forms part of The National Forest *Grange Walk* (see the section on The National Forest for details). This is a 14 mile long distance walk that links historic houses, former coal mines, and new woodlands to the active New Cliffe Quarry. The route aims to celebrate the industrial heritage of the area and its future as part of the evolving National Forest.

The larger quarry at Billa Barra Hill.

New Cliffe Hill Quarry

The path opens out at the top to give a good panoramic view of the southern face of New Cliffe Hill Quarry. Walk up to the viewing platform to get a bird's-eye view into the quarry **(3)**.

Please note that the quarry is dangerous. Do not venture from the path or attempt to enter the quarry at any point along the route; there are unexpected vertical drops to the quarry floor.

The first thing that you will notice when looking into the quarry is the huge U-shaped feature in the back wall of the quarry in front of you. This is a cross-section through an ancient Triassic **wadi** or desert river valley. During flash floods, a large quantity of sediment and rock waste would be eroded from the wadi floor and sides to be transported and eventually redeposited when the raging torrent subsided.

The reddish brown sedimentary rocks that infill the wadi in front of you are the Triassic *Mercia Mudstones*; they consist of red silty mudstone with scattered greenish grey bands and patches. The red coloration, mud cracks and evaporite deposits found within the mudstone all indicate deposition in an arid **desert** climate. The red colour is due to a thin coating of the iron oxide **hematite** around the grains that make up the sedimentary rock.

The wadi channel cuts down into a dark grey coloured igneous rock known as the *South Charnwood Diorite*. The diorite is considered to be late Precambrian in age, and is thought to have intruded into the older Charnian rocks; evidence for this will be examined in the Old Cliffe Hill section. Thin sections or 'slices' of rock examined under a microscope show that the diorite mainly consists of plagioclase feldspar, augite and quartz, with abundant secondary alteration products epidote, chlorite and calcite. However, the most

The Triassic wadi channel cuts down into the Precambrian South Charnwood Diorite, New Cliffe Hill Quarry.

distinctive feature of the diorite is the abundance of **granophyre** — a runic or cuniform intergrowth of quartz and feldspar.

Notice the difference between the two rock types: the diorites are a very uniform dark grey colour, with a 'blocky' jointed nature. The Triassic rocks in contrast are a brighter reddish brown colour, and gently dipping bedding is clearly defined. Stepped ledges on the quarry walls in the diorite are benches cut during removal of rock from the steep quarry face. The interpretation sketch below picks out the main features of each rock type.

The irregular surface that separates the two very different lithologies is known as an **unconformity**, and represents a 'gap' in time from the Precambrian to the Triassic; hence it is known as the *Triassic unconformity*. The unconformity surface is marked by a thin breccia horizon that passes rapidly upwards into the *Mercia Mudstone*. Triassic breccias are thought to infill depressions in the irregular Triassic land surface, and are very localised in occurrence. The breccia on the unconformity surface at Cliffe Hill is also host to some

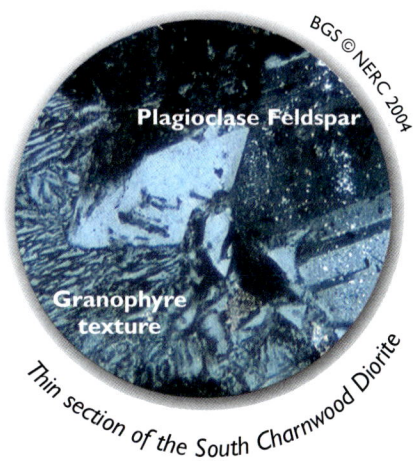

Thin section of the South Charnwood Diorite

important and unusual minerals, including the copper minerals cuprite, azurite, malachite and native copper as well as strontium, barytes and vanadium.

> It is thought that the highest hills of Charnwood Forest were formerly covered by Triassic *Mercia Mudstone*, which suggests that the Triassic deposits were originally much thicker than they are today. In the western part of this district, an even greater thickness of Triassic sediment accumulated in the subsiding *Hinckley Basin* just to the east of Nuneaton. Gravity models indicate that in the centre of the Hinckley Basin at least 500 m of *Mercia Mudstone* is preserved, which probably only represents about half of their original thickness.

It is difficult to discern any structure to the diorites from a distance apart from the blocky joint surfaces. However, steeply dipping fractures or **shear zones** can be seen in the diorite below the wadi channel.

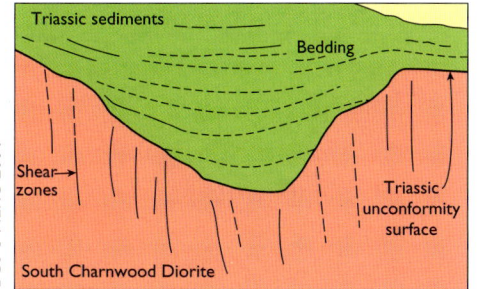

Interpretative sketch of the Triassic wadi channel.

One theory is that the Triassic rivers cut down preferentially into the diorite where the fractures or shear zones are found, as these structures represent localised zones of weakness in the otherwise resistant crystalline bedrock. Consequently, Triassic wadi channels and shear zones in the diorite tend to be found together in the same locality.

Chalky Till, deposited by an ice sheet in Pleistocene times (the Ice Age: about half a million years ago) can be seen in the exposed bluffs near the road, on the left hand side of the quarry. Secondary alteration has occurred where reducing solutions have infiltrated through these glacial sediments. If such solutions enter the sediments through porous horizons, or through cracks and fractures in the rock, the orangey coloration is then locally altered to a pale green, grey or even white colour. Such **redox** fronts can be seen in the Pleistocene sediments to the left of the quarry.

The picture below gives an idea of the type of animal that wandered the glacial landscape during the great Ice Age, or Pleistocene period.

A woolly mammoth roams the glacial plains during the Ice Age.

Look carefully at the walls of the viewing platform;

they are made up entirely from rock gathered from both Old and New Cliffe Hill Quarry. These rocks allow you to get a closer look at the lithology and geological history of the formations that you can see from afar in the quarry. The main rock types in the walls include:

1) Green and pink speckled rocks — the *South Charnwood Diorite*. The viewing platform walls are made up mainly of this rock, as New Cliffe Hill Quarry is composed predominantly of diorite.

Notice the vivid bright green–turquoise coloration on some of the diorites; this is the result of copper mineralisation. Perhaps these specimens came from close to the unconformity surface. Other minerals include **epidote** (a pale pistachio green) and iron oxides such as the 'blood red' coloured mineral **hematite**.

Some of the diorites in the wall have flat polished surfaces with elongated streaks running across them; run your finger-tips across the streaks to feel their grooved texture. These are **slickenside** lines developed as a result of movement across the shear zones cutting through the diorite. Quartz veins or **tension gashes** can also be seen crossing some of the diorites.

2) Dark greenish grey–purple layered rocks — the *Bradgate Formation*. (Table 1) There are few examples of

the *Bradgate Formation* in the walls of the viewing platform; you will need to look very carefully for this rock type. There is only a very small exposure of the *Bradgate Formation* on the north-western side of this quarry, which unfortunately cannot be seen from the viewing platform. At New Cliffe Hill the formation consists of variably bedded tuffs and coarser grained tuffs and agglomerates. The *Bradgate Formation* can be seen more clearly in the sheer walls of the Old Cliffe Hill Quarry. Unfortunately, this quarry is currently inaccessible, but an interpretation board located on the footpath to the north-west of Old Cliffe Hill Quarry **(5)** displays a geological map of the quarry and describes the rocks in more detail.

The village of Stanton under Bardon. The earth embankment (bund) surrounding Old Cliffe Hill Quarry can be seen behind the village.

After looking into the quarry void, turn around (with your back to the quarry) with Billa Barra Hill in front of you. The wooded hill with the radio masts to your left (to the north) is Bardon Hill, thought to be the closest point to the volcanic centre in Precambrian times.

Turn back around to look into the quarry again. Turn left and follow the footpath skirting the quarry, towards the south-east. Midland Quarry Products replaced the public footpaths, diverted when quarrying began, and completed a footpath link between Battleflat Lane and Stanton village. Residents named this route the 'Quarryman's Way' in a competition organised by the Company in 1997.

After a few 100 m's you will notice the earth bund surrounding Old Cliffe Hill Quarry and the village of Stanton under Bardon on your left. Continue following the footpath next to the fence, between the trees as it starts to descend away from the quarry edge. After crossing the little wooden footbridge and stile, turn right, and then right again to cross another wooden footbridge on to the 'Quarryman's Way' This will lead you back to the edge of the quarry through the plantation of trees. Continue on to point **(4)** on the map, which affords a good view of the northern face of the quarry and the quarry workings.

> As you walk, notice the broadleaf trees beyond the perimeter fence, planted by Midland Quarry Products in association with the National Forest Company, to landscape the area around the edge of the quarry void. At points along this walk you will have good views over the fence into the deep quarry workings. Again, please do not stray from the footpath to get a closer view!

A Circuit around New Cliffe Hill

If you would like to walk the full circuit of this footpath around the quarry, continue following the perimeter fence until you return to the viewing platform at point **(3)** (approximately an extra 3.3 km). The walk from this point onwards is not particularly scenic and there are no more good views of the quarry. However you will be able to see the quarry processing plant more clearly and the quarry settlement ponds that were created when New Cliffe Hill was established. When the earthwork embankments were being constructed at the quarry, the water that ran off these areas was too silty to be released into the nearby rivers. The quarry company therefore created ponds to enable the silt to settle out of suspension. Now that the embankments are grassed, silt from the run off is negligible. As a result, the ponds now form an important local wetland habitat, and are a haven for wildlife.

If you decide to walk the circular route, when you reach the viewing platform at point **(3)** again, you can either:

i) Return to and walk past the Billa Barra car park and turn right at the main road. After approximately 250 m, cross the road and look out for a footpath sign (*Ivanhoe Way*) off to the left. An interpretation board (at point **(5)**) on the footpath describes the geology of Old Cliffe Hill Quarry (currently inaccessible).

ii) Alternatively, you could stay on the footpath skirting the quarry lip, and follow directions to the village of Stanton (described below).

From point **(4)**, retrace your steps and cross over the wooden footbridge. Turn right onto the footpath, and cross the stiles. Walk straight on through the field and past the metal gate. Continue straight on until you meet the main road (Thornton Lane) through the village of Stanton under Bardon.

If you would like to visit the local pub, turn right and walk downhill for approximately 400 m — the *Old Thatched Inn* can be found on the left at the bottom of the hill. Food is available (please phone for times). There is also a small playground at the back of the primary school en route to the pub, where children can let off steam.

Alternatively, turn left at the main road to visit the local shop and post office to buy refreshments and snacks (approximately 50 m on the left). There is also a bus stop at this point. Telephone Traveline (0870 6082608) for details of times and routes.

View over the rolling countryside of the North-West Leicestershire Coalfield, from the walk around New Cliffe Hill Quarry.

Old Cliffe Hill Quarry

Aerial photograph of Old Cliffe Hill Quarry (This image is an extract from the Millenium Map, which is copyright to getmapping plc).

Walk up the main street through Stanton under Bardon to the T-junction with the Cliffe Hill Road; turn left, and cross the road at a safe point. Look out for a footpath on the right after approximately 50 m (*Ivanhoe Way*). You will see an interpretation board near the intersection of the footpath and the main road **(5)**, on which you will find more information on the geology of Old Cliffe Hill. The quarry is currently inaccessible as Old Cliffe Hill is now entering into a new phase of excavation from 2004, in order to work the remaining reserves. The map on the interpretation board provides an idea of the geology of the quarry.

Old Cliffe Hill Quarry is, like New Cliffe Hill, composed mainly of the dark grey *South Charnwood Diorite*. However, important exposures of the *Bradgate Formation* are found at Old Cliffe Hill, outcropping along the north and eastern edge of the quarry. Typically, the *Bradgate Formation* consists of green to purple-grey finely laminated volcaniclastic mudstone and siltstone. These beds are shown to be water lain by the wide range of sedimentary structures that they contain, including graded bedding, erosional scour surfaces and channels. Contorted, deformed and slumped beds are also present. It is thought that the sediments were deformed soon after deposition as a result of **earthquake activity**.

The sediments of the *Bradgate Formation* represent a **turbidite** succession, deposited from a fast flowing current of water in which sediment is kept in suspension through the turbulence of the water (hence 'turbidity current') Deposition occurs when the turbidity current slows down. Paradoxically, the rare Precambrian fossils have been found in the uppermost parts of the turbidite beds in the *Bradgate Formation*. The fossils were probably transported in this current from their original life-sites. At the eastern end of Old Cliffe Hill Quarry, examples of the Ediacaran fossil *Cyclomedusa Cliffii* have been found as impressions on bedding planes (Figure 1).

At Old Cliffe Hill Quarry, there is evidence that hot molten diorite was intruded into

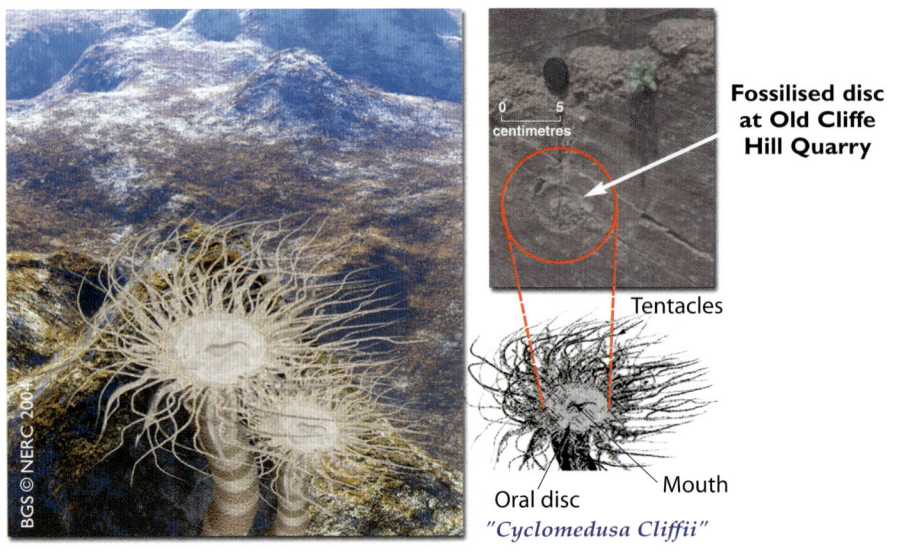

Figure 1 *The Ediacaran organism — Cyclomedusa Cliffii.*

the older volcaniclastic tuffs of the *Bradgate Formation*. The diorite is seen to darken and become more finely grained towards the contact with the tuffs. This is indicative of chilling as the diorite cooled down as it intruded into the tuff. The tuffs are also bleached to a pale cream colour within centimetres of the contact. They also have developed small thermal spots as a result of chemical changes due to the proximity of the hot diorite.

The *Triassic Mercia Mudstone* is also to be found at Old Cliffe Hill Quarry, lying unconformably above the older diorite and tuffs of the *Bradgate Formation*. The unconformity can be traced all around the quarry, and overlying it the Triassic red beds are draped, effectively 'filling in' the pre-Triassic land topography.

Return to the main road, turn right and walk for approximately 250 m, then turn left and immediate right, back to the Billa Barra car park.

If you would like a refreshment stop at the service station on the M1 round-about, turn left out of the car park and left again onto Stanton Lane. After approximately 500 m, turn right at the roundabout, towards Markfield and Groby (the *Flying Horse* pub is on the right hand side). Continue on this road to the large roundabout (M1/A50 junction), where you will see the services located on the right; there are several fast-food restaurants, a shop and toilets at the services.

OLD CLIFFE HILL QUARRY 21

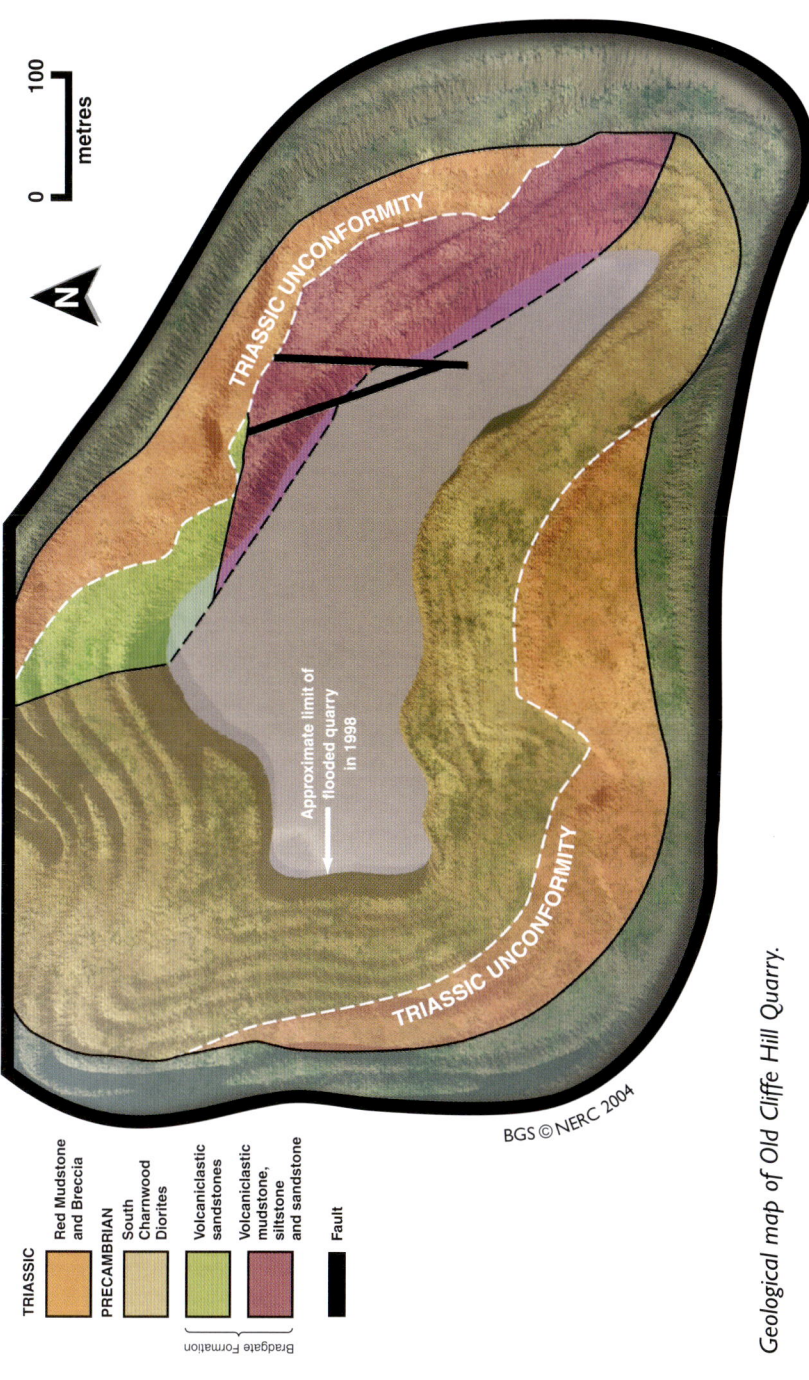

Geological map of Old Cliffe Hill Quarry.

Hill Hole Quarry

Hill Hole Quarry, Markfield

Parking can be found at several places in Markfield to gain access to Hill Hole Quarry — either in the car park on Hill Lane, or on the road near to the Parish Church of St Michael and All Angels. The former car park will give quick access to the quarry, while parking near the church is more interesting historically.

At the M1 roundabout take the A50 exit (signposted to Leicester) and after several hundred metres take the left filter lane towards the village of Markfield (signed for Shepshed and Markfield). At the end of the road turn left and follow signs to Markfield, passing over the motorway bridge. If you decide to park on **Hill Lane (6)** take the second right (signposted 'Industrial Estate') onto Hill Lane. After 200 m, turn left on to the car park. There are various new footpaths into the quarry from the car park.

If you prefer to park near the **church (7)**, do not turn right, but continue straight on, past the *Queens Head* pub, and take the first right onto Main Street. Continue on this road and take the third road on the right, on to 'The Green'. The Parish Church of St Michael and All Angels can be found at the top of the hill; park anywhere near the church.

Please note: The following route starts from the church.

The church is built of *South Charnwood Diorite* (or '*Markfieldite*') from the nearby quarry. However, the roof is not tiled with the Cambrian *Swithland Slate*, which tends to be the favoured roofing material in older buildings around the Charnwood area. *Swithland Slates* were actually used as roofing materials by the Romans in Leicester, but by the 18th century the industry had grown and *Swithland Slate* was used for roofing houses and for headstones, milestones, sundials, gateposts and for some household items. However, with the improvement of transportation, the slate industry expanded in the 19th century, and cheaper Welsh slate then flooded the market. The Welsh slates were easier to split, and produced a more refined, lighter slate tile. As a result the local Swithland Slate Industry went into a rapid decline.

If you have time, enjoy a quick walk around the church and graveyard. Notice the small brick-built house (date 1771) abutting the church lych gate; both are

HILL HOLE QUARRY

Compare the 'rough' Swithland Slates of the lych gate to the more precisely cut Welsh slates on the roof of the church behind.

On leaving the churchyard, turn left and walk uphill. On passing the church keep to the right, and walk to the end of the road where you will find a metal swing gate. After approximately 20 m, take the very small overgrown path on your left, leading steeply uphill. The track bends around to the right after 30 m, again steeply uphill directly to the quarry lip **(please note this path may have been improved since writing)**. A set of stone and gravel steps descend to the quarry floor (the main quarry void is fenced off for safety).

roofed with *Swithland Slate*. A plaque on the house wall reads 'the Reverend John Wesley (1703–1791) preached in the church and outside during 13 visits 1741–1779'. At this point you can compare the rather rough, speckly grey-coloured *Swithland Slates* on the lych gate roof, with the smoother, more precisely cut Welsh slates on the church roof. There is an interesting mix of multi coloured slate headstones in the churchyard, some of which were quarried locally.

The church itself dates back in part to the 12th century, although it was extensively altered in the 19th century. Inside, look out for the interesting stained glass windows, the 'Porritt' organ, the stone font and the cheeky gargoyle heads supporting the base of each of the arched wooden roof beams. The carpet apparently covers the tomb of a George Herine (died in 1718), who is said to have been the son of the illustrious King of the Gypsies.

The quarry **(8)** is composed entirely of the *South Charnwood Diorite*, as seen and described earlier at New Cliffe Hill Quarry. Notice the rounded and blocky jointed nature of the diorite. The quarry first opened in the 1860s, but was abandoned before the First World War. A windmill stood on Markfield Hill before 1743, but the site was unfortunately quarried away by the 1870s. The quarry was bought by Hinckley and Bosworth Borough Council with grant aid from the National Forest Company. The site supports a variety of unusual flora and fauna, including a rare type of lichen, only found at one other site in Leicestershire, and a rare variety of spider. There is also a protected species of rare white-clawed crayfish within the lake, the only species of freshwater crayfish native to the UK. Hill Hole Quarry has a host of new footpaths providing easy access around the site, and is a great spot for short walk and picnic. Rock climbing in the quarry is strictly controlled.

Blacksmith's Field

It is possible to walk (or drive) from Hill Hole Quarry to the Blacksmiths Field and Altar Stones sites. On leaving by the Hill Lane exit, turn right and walk or drive for approximately 400 to 500 m past the industrial estate. Turn left at the T-junction and immediately left again into Ashby Road (signposted 'Altar Stones Playing Fields'). Walk for a further 250 to 300 m; the Blacksmith's Field site can be found on the right of the road (9). If you parked near the church, retrace your steps back along Main Street and turn left at the T-junction. After approximately 400 m, turn left onto Ashby Road following the sign for 'Altar Stones Playing Fields'. The Blacksmith's Field site can be found after 100 m on the right hand side of the road. The Altar Stones site is 100 m farther on (10). Parking is acceptable on the roadside, or in the lay-by next to the Altar Stones site.

The 2.25 ha site was bought by the Leicestershire and Rutland Wildlife Trust with grant aid from the National Forest Company, Leicestershire County Council and Hinckley and Bosworth Borough Council. Blacksmith's Field is classed as a Regionally Important Geological Site, on the basis of the outcrops of the *Bradgate Formation*, thought to be around 550 to 580 million years old. This formation can also be seen at Billa Barra Hill, and is composed mainly of volcaniclastic sediment or tuff. The reserve is named after a blacksmith's shop that once existed on the site. It is also thought that the area was quarried in the late 19th century.

The habitat is predominantly heath grassland with some scattered scrub and some acid grassland. There are three small ponds, overgrown with willow and rush. Rare lichens of national importance can also be found on the dry stone walls and on the rock outcrops.

There is an interpretation board providing more information at the entrance to the site. It is a nice spot to have a picnic, followed by a quick walk through the crags.

A rare variety of spider from Hill Hole Quarry.

Altar Stones

This 1.21 ha site is owned by the Leicestershire County Council and managed by the Country Parks service. The site, which was gifted to the County Council in 1949, is noted for its craggy rock outcrops, and is another lovely spot for a short walk and picnic. It is thought that the Altar Stones site was historically a place for ancient Druid worship. The name could also have been derived from the 'auter' stones, an old term meaning 'outer' stones.

The Altar Stones are classed as a Regionally Important Geological Site (RIGS), and have important outcrops of the *Bradgate Formation*. They also contain the finer grained *Beacon Hill Tuff* and an exposure of the *Sliding Stone Slump Breccia*, which is an important marker horizon for Charnwood Forest. A spectacular exposure of the type section of the *Sliding Stone Slump Breccia* can be seen at Bradgate Park, accessed from the Hunt's Hill car park in Newtown Linford. **For further information please see 'A Geological walk around Bradgate Park and Swithland Wood' (this series).** Grassy paths provide walks between the stones and the two small ponds; there are good views over the ancient Charnwood Forest. The area surrounding the Altar Stones supports heath and gorse.

The area was once the site of an old post mill, Markfield's second windmill. Look out for the dilapidated remains of the miller's store near the bottom of the road. The windmill itself blew down in a storm in 1895.

Sunset behind the Altar Stones — a site of ancient Druid worship...

Photograph: A McGrath

The National Forest

Britain's most ambitious environmental endeavour!

In the very Heart of England, across parts of Leicestershire, Derbyshire and Staffordshire, some 200 square miles of town and countryside is being transformed, blending ancient woodland with new planting to create a multi-purpose forest for the nation on a scale not seen in this country for over a thousand years; it is a forest in the making. Nearly six million trees have already been planted and, ultimately 30 million trees will create stunning new landscapes and wildlife habitats, for the benefit of the community, countryside and environment.

The National Forest & Beyond *Where to go and what to do 2004* (attractions leaflet) and *Places to stay and things to do 2004* (visitor guide) provide further information on sites, attractions and places to stay in and around The National Forest.

Sites and visitor attractions that could be combined with the walk around Cliffe Hill Quarry include:

Martins Wood and Martinshaw Wood, Woodhouse Eaves.

Beacon Hill Country Park has views over Leicestershire, and a Bronze Age hill fort.

Burroughs Wood, a site blending new and ancient woodland.

Thornton Reservoir, a 75 acre reservoir set amongst rolling farmland and woodland. There is a fishing lodge and trails for walkers, cyclists and the disabled.

Donington le Heath Manor House, a medieval manor house dating back to 1280.

THE NATIONAL FOREST   27

The National Forest Walks Guide — a full colour guide to 15 walks in The National Forest, ranging from 3 to 22 miles in length. The guide includes information on features of interest and facilities for each walk and comes in a handy A5 loose-leaf file. Available from the National Forest Company, Tourist Information Centres, and other attractions across the area, price £5.

For further information on The National Forest, for details of forest sites close to Midland Quarry Products, Cliffe Hill Quarry, or for details of all National Forest leaflets and guides see contact details below.

© National Forest Company

The National Forest Walks Guide.

Location map of The National Forest.

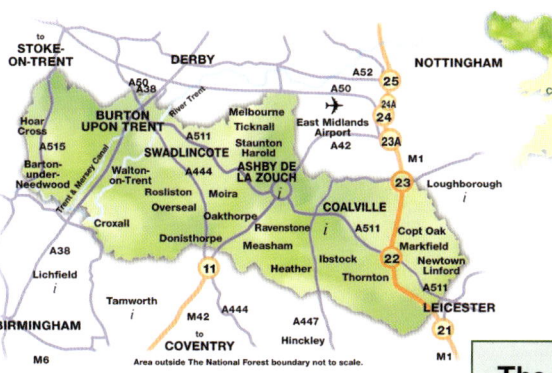

Photograph: R Fraser

**The National Forest Company,
Enterprise Glade,
Bath Lane, Moira,
Swadlincote,
Derbyshire DE12 6BD**

Tel: 01283 551211
Fax: 01283 552844

Website: www.nationalforest.org
Email: enquiries@nationalforest.org